skin splitting

poems

poems by

Bryanna Licciardi

Finishing Line Press
Georgetown, Kentucky

skin splitting

poems

Copyright © 2017 by Bryanna Licciardi
ISBN 978-1-63534-296-3 First Edition
All rights reserved under International and Pan-American Copyright Conventions.
No part of this book may be reproduced in any manner whatsoever without written
permission from the publisher, except in the case of brief quotations embodied in critical
articles and reviews.

Publisher: Leah Maines

Editor: Christen Kincaid

Cover Art: Matt Watkins

Author Photo: William Grainger

Printed in the USA on acid-free paper.
Order online: www.finishinglinepress.com
also available on amazon.com

Author inquiries and mail orders:
Finishing Line Press
P. O. Box 1626
Georgetown, Kentucky 40324
U. S. A.

Table of Contents

Naked 1

Why We Aren't Animals 2

At a Party, John Wayne Gacy puts his Arm around me and Says
    We've all been there Before 4

Pack 6

We Normally Avoid Scotty's House 7

On Leaving the Green River Killer 8

Pair Bonds 10

The Angel Makers and I Try to Bake a Cake 11

On Learning I am the Bully 12

Parasomnia 13

Someone Sets me up with Charles Manson 14

Skinned 15

Floating, Sinking 16

The French Ripper Takes me to a Hot Dog Stand 18

Trying to Reason with the Baby I Never Plan to Have 19

Specimen 20

Jeffrey Dahmer Invites me to a Dinner Party 21

I Put Her Back Under my Floor 23

The Grim Sleeper Takes me Hiking Before his Execution 24

Perspective 25

Sunday Morning Slasher Dies on a Friday, My Letter Doesn't
    Arrive 'til Monday 27

Your Friendly Female Anthropologist's Take on Bar Pick-Ups 28

Bucket List 30

Losing Weight 31

naked

In church, I dream of Marilyn Monroe, stepping on and over pews so
worshippers could gaze up her skirt. She wants them to see what made her

like every other girl. Such nakedness mesmerizes all of us here.
When I try to worship my own body, it's not like hers. Mine feels
too exposed, too exploited

by flaws I've collected over the years
like fridge magnets that hold fixed reminders of doctor notes,
cellulite, surgical scars, freckles, to pick up the *diet* soda

because these thighs are wide enough. They tell me I am
no Marilyn. In church, I have dreams of her walking toward me
down the center aisle.

Her nakedness always moves me
out of my seat.

why we aren't animals

Sharks are resistant to cancer
the way you are to hot water.
I remember our first shower, and
your hands, how I let my skin burn
so you wouldn't stop.

> A giraffe's heart can weigh
> over twenty pounds.
> I think of its weight
> when we go to bed mad,

and I think of your rock-hard tongue,
of your teeth grinding in my ears at night.
I want to be an ant that never sleeps,
a dolphin keeping watch with one eye.

> The pig can scarcely look up, its neck
> designed to keep him low and facing the ground.

Tonight, it's raining. I try to keep my gaze high without blinking.
There's something inscrutable about the sky.

> Owls are the only birds that can see
> the color blue—the color that looks best on you.

Female stick bugs reproduce almost entirely
without males. Only the male cricket chirps.

> There was a life in you that's missing now,
> that you threw to the dogs—
> maybe long before we met.

The Cretan hound is the rarest breed of dog.
I imagine a pack of them running you down
and tearing you to pieces,
gnawing what's left of you
between the bones.

But then again, if we were perfect,
there would be no need for love.

at a party, john wayne gacy puts his arm around me and says we've all been there before

"When he killed, he sometimes dressed as his alter ego 'Pogo the Clown.'"
-From a biography of the infamous serial killer

He smells like tequila
and I have no idea
what he's talking about,
but since he's drunk
and so am I,
I let him refill my glass.
You're in the next room.
I can't see you, but
your loud laugh carries
around the corner.
I wonder if you're telling that joke
about the funeral parlor's
layaway plan,
or if you're flirting with
an older woman
who reminds you of your mother.
John looks like he's asked a question,
like he's waiting for me to answer.
For the first time,
I notice a tall hat on his head
tilted towards me,
his face painted up
like a sad clown.
With each sip he takes, the red smears
a little more around his lips.
He's still waiting,
so I say, *Absolutely.*
I guess it's the right answer
because he grins, grabs my hand,
and starts pulling me
through the crowd. As we pass,
the partygoers drop dead.
Their bodies make music against the floor,
soft and rhythmic.

He's leading me up the stairs,
and, though I look back,
I can't think of a reason to stop him.

pack

May 21, 1908

Spliced together early this morning, Frank,
the world's first two-headed dog,

owes much to the scientific resourcefulness
of a Dr. Charles Claude Guthrie.

Dr. Guthrie says he implanted the newest edition
upside down, so the two could look at each other

and share intimacies only two heads can.
Frank lived for approximately seven hours.

Proof of life was the single tear produced by one head,
and the lapping of it by the other's tongue.

Dr. Guthrie was shocked to later learn this experiment cost him
the Nobel, said next time, he'd be sure to use purebreds.

we normally avoid scotty's house

But today we decide to chuck rocks at his door,
watching as they sparkle midair before
we run for cover. They hit with sharp, small force.
When Scotty comes out, we duck,
pressed tight against his neighbor's car.

Our hands try to smother laughter. We count
one, two, waiting to get caught, *nine, ten…*
The brave one, I peek over the hood and see him
standing on his porch, eyes already on me in his
dirty-white shirt and bare feet. I run,

abandoning my friend who, for reasons
perhaps beginning here, would not be
my friend for long. Scotty has called by the time
I make it home. I know this as soon as I see Dad
pacing our driveway, and then, wrist-grabbed,

I'm dragged back the way I ran. Dad says
he's ashamed. He says I need Scotty's forgiveness.
The whole way back, I'm thinking this is it.
This is how I die. Delivered right to hands of
our creepy neighbor who still lives with his mom,

grandma, too. Just one knock and Scotty appears,
obscurely framed by his doorway. A sour smell seeps
from inside. I try to appear calm, but up close,
his dark red beard looks like flames licking at his face,
the way his smile, undisturbed, seems to lick at mine.

on leaving the green river killer

"I would talk to her... and get her mind off of the, sex, anything she was nervous about. And think, you know, she thinks, 'Oh, this guy cares'... which I didn't. I just want to, uh, get her in the vehicle and eventually kill her."
　　　　　–Gary Ridgway discussing his victims
　　　　　Convicted of 48 murder counts in 2003

When we fight, he calls me
sweet things like honey

and sugar bear,
doesn't think I notice the way

he crosses his arms
tighter and tighter, which

makes me think if he
crosses them any more

he'll disappear
and I'll be screaming

about the kids we never had
to an empty room, though

I'm really screaming about
what made him want

those women more than
me. And when he leaves

to pour us a glass of beer,
I think this is my chance,

I think this me walking out,
but instead I sit down,

angry in knowing that
before he even comes back,

he'll have undone a few buttons,
he'll be smiling.

pair bonds

"Among foxes a pair-bond lasts only through the breeding season."
–Helen Fisher, Anatomy of Love

I imagine this is how it goes:

In the beginning, they lick and kiss
each other's face. He brings home only

the best meat.   He promises their lives together
will be unflappable and fervent, their love just as it

always has, until his hunts grow longer.
Distractions, overnight trips, coming around less

and less, and, in the end, never again.
Taken over by desperate shame,

the female fox drives away her children.
They've become a constant reminder.

the angel makers and I try to bake a cake

"Rumours of the Wholesale 'Removal' of Unwanted Husbands Start the Authorities to Open Dozens of Graves in the Village Church Yard at Nagyrev, Hungary, With Startling Results"
                      -1929 headline of the Nagyrev village's serial killer group

I'm not sure whose kitchen we're in,
because all of the wives seem to belong here.
Counters are covered with flour and tonic bottles.
No one talks, yet they all move together
in unison, one setting down an empty cup
for another to fill with sugar, and yet another
picks it up to mix in to the milk and eggs.
Some arrive late and some leave during.
Some stare at me like they want to tell me
I don't belong. When I try to get closer to
the bowl, the woman stirring throws out
a sharp arm. *No,* she says. *This is no place for
a single woman.* But you promised to show me,
I say, which makes her laugh. Instead, she offers
the spoon, daring me to lick off the batter.
All of the other women laugh, too, so I step back.
Good choice, she says, then tosses the spoon in
the trash, along with the bowl, and all of the batter.

on learning I am the bully

Normally I can look away, but today one of the girls
hands me a willow branch, says in a low voice,
Whip that nerd. Arlie's coming by again
on her bike with the training wheels. She was my
best friend until the other girls invited me around.
Seeing her now, I'm mad she doesn't care what
they think. I'm jealous she doesn't try hard, like me.
With the branch I run after her, swinging,
trying to ignore the way she cries out,
the sharp sound it makes against her skin.
I want to take it back even as I'm doing it,
but I keep hitting her until she rides off.

After that, her mom keeps Arlie away from me.
I stop by each day, letting her send me away.
I'm scared of what I did, but don't get why,
or don't want to, so I keep knocking,
and ignore the older girls who've started
laughing at me, too, until finally, weeks later,
Arlie answers the door with her mom.

We spend the afternoon in her backyard
sketching butterflies as they eat from her feeder.
They never stay still enough for me,
but Arlie can draw them from memory.
I watch her tiny, pale fingers expertly
pull the pencil around the page
and as I open my mouth to say something
she looks up at me and smiles.
I don't know how she did it,
but I don't want her to take it back,
so I smile, too. When the butterflies leave,
Arlie and I climb into the garden bed,
where we dig up rolie polies
and watch them curl up in our hands.

parasomnia

"...what he wanted seemed to have too many corners to come out of his mouth."
    –Stephen King, Roadwork

Sometimes I dream of children in this house, and their tiny fingers
are made of paper. They sneak behind me, smother my mouth until
I have to chew my way out. Sometimes I wake up crouched

in the corner, terrified they've followed me out, their fingers
still like ghosts against my mouth. Sometimes I go to bed
holding scissors, just in case next time they don't want me alive.

Sometimes I don't want out. Sometimes they're kind. They've built
me this house. Their delicate fingers took time to crease the corners
of each papered room. Sometimes they're my children, and they

tell me about our family history, of the children my children will have
some day. Sometimes we circle a paper fireplace, lit softly in the corner
of this house, which is ours. They take turns admiring my fingers,

because their own are dimensionless, ask me what a cut feels like,
or a burn, and I say, *Like it's not supposed to be there.* Sometimes
the paper is black, not white, and the house is too dark. Sometimes

running into, and through our walls, I search for them, but they're gone.
Sometimes they search for me. And with paper mouths, sometimes
their cries have too many corners to make it past their throats.

someone sets me up with charles manson

Charles Manson, notorious for the murders of the famous actress Sharon Tate and other Hollywood residents, is one of the few serial killers who was never actually found guilty of committing a murder himself.

But I get there to find Charles has sent two guys in his place. They eat like wolves and want me to pay because Charles told them I would, and I do. I ask if he'll show up later, and they tell me, maybe, but he's Manson, Son of Men—so it's hard to say. The taller guy puts his hand on my knee and winks. The other one, gnashing meat through his teeth when he smiles, has a southern accent and asks me to call him Cowboy. Eventually I make an excuse to leave, can't recall why I even showed, but they follow me into my car and fling off their shoes. I have to roll down the windows it smells so bad. Where can I drop you off, I say. What's the rush, they want to know. Cowboy asks if I'd like to see their ranch, learn about the coming war, and possibly bang The Man himself. I've finally discovered my sanity, so I tell them when pigs fly and the tall one says, Oh, they may not fly, but boy do we make them run.

skinned

When I take my cat
for a checkup,
the vet finds he's gained
ten pounds
this year alone.
Her tone is reproachful,
concerned, sincere.

My mother,
blind in one eye,
sees half of me
and still tells me
I'm beautiful,

but my skin is impure.
I scrub it every day.
The backs of my
arms and legs
becoming brittle.
See my bones surface,
rising into my skin
that cannot hold.
See I am breakable.
I will not last this way.

In the checkout line
with my cart of premium
diet cat food, I try to avoid
everyone's eye, anyone
quick to guess how I've
ruined my cat's health.
Until the boy at the register
offers me a tissue,
I don't notice I've been
scratching my arm, or that
it's started to bleed.

floating, sinking

After he's gone, my dreams are filled with rivers.
I raft downstream, tasting salt in the air, the mist,
searching for an ocean that never comes.
The current always steady and slow,
the light so dull I can barely see.
Sometimes I try to stand. Sometimes I jump off.

Last year my dog of seven years slips off
his leash and runs towards the river
at the bottom of the hill. I see
my dad disappear after him in the mist.
It's almost an hour before he returns walking slow
and empty-handed, becoming

slower still when he reaches me. Then my mom comes
around the corner, wiping off
her hands with a dish towel. She slows,
seeing something in his face. *The river...*
he starts. We look back into the mist,
but he says nothing else. For months, I refuse to see

what happened in this silence. You can't see
something if you turn away. When he doesn't come
back, I stay quiet to prolong my dog in mystery. I miss
him, but saying so will send him further away. I keep death off
my street, imagining it waiting on the banks of the river,
fear at night waving into me slowly.

Today, I'm learning how to swim but I'm slow,
slower than the other kids. I see
them swim past me stronger, faster, and the pool is a river
I let take me. Sinking deeper, I try to welcome
the knowledge that some things are better off dead.
I don't realize I'm screaming until Mister

Hendricks, the teacher, tries to lift me from the mist.
He pulls, but it won't let go of me. He tells me to slow

my breathing, but I can't because I'm off
this wet pavement and slipping still. I can see
pity and fear in his far-away face. Then come
the floods, waves crash over me, the river

and the mist rising, pouring me into a dark-mouthed sea,
whose gnash and grind of teeth slow down only after skin comes
off my body, and his, and all the others floating in this river.

the french ripper takes me to a hot dog stand

Considered the French's version of Jack the Ripper, Joseph Vacher's scarred face, and white hand-sewn rabbit fur hat made for quite a spectacle during trial, as did his insanity plea. He was executed in 1898 via guillotine for the murder of 11 people.

When I say I'm a vegetarian, he laughs,
devours the dog in three bites, licks
the ketchup from between his fingers.
He says he's come to me like Jesus,
like Joan of Arc, come to us all
to guide his beloved flock to
the slaughterhouse. I ask
what his beheading was like,
and he gets serious, scratches at
the scar across his neck.
He asserts it to be
the most honorable way to die.
Then why try to get out of it, I ask.
Joseph stops me dead
in my tracks, takes off his furry
hat and places it on my head.
Nearly as good, he says.
I pet it as we continue walking,
and I must admit that,
once you get used to the smell,
and the stains, it's almost
like wearing a crown.

trying to reason with the baby I never plan to have

Know that it takes one thousand days to detox
and my weekly trip to the winery is unavoidable.
Know that big heads run in my family, that a baby's head
makes up 25 percent of its length, that Einstein's brain
was 15 percent wider than normal and you would definitely be
smarter than Einstein. Know that Americans are over-eaters,
that you'd probably be obese because my cat is obese,
and because I eat when I'm upset.

Know that aliens like to abduct babies at night,
that I sleep with the windows open, that aliens run
in my family, that girls have faster heartbeats,
boys blink less, that unlike other humans, identical twins
have the same exact scent, that babies are born with
100 extra bones, and I can't decide which one of those facts
freaks me out more.

Know that people live better without food than sleep,
that babies don't understand the concept of night and day,
that I have to go to bed by 8 o'clock or I'm no good,
that high levels of testosterone make you feel pleasure
from inflicting pain, that testosterone runs in my family.
Know that anger increases people's desire to possess things,
and I can barely share a bottle of wine, that I've been known
to hide it before company arrives.

Know that having you would eat at least 20 percent
of my salary, that by not having you, I can avoid the wage gap,
and though people see my empty womb as proof of lesbianism,
or alienism, I'm okay with that. Know that you'd be able to hear
my voice in the womb, and I can't sing worth a damn.
Know that if you died, hearing would be your last sense to go.
That if the heart stops before the brain, you might still
hear me saying your name.

specimen

My frog's skin splits like silk
beneath the scalpel,
thin fingers palmed up
towards me. Its insides
are rotting grey.
Something isn't right,

so I call over the teacher.
*Where's the heart
supposed to be?*
He says that is seems
my specimen was pregnant,
uses a blade to scoop up her eggs.

Running to the restroom,
I scrub my hands with soap
but the smell only grows stronger,
and I know I'll fail the exam
because there's no way to decipher
what in her body is not death.

jeffrey dahmer invites me to a dinner party

Before eating and ultimately dismembering his victims, he'd often sedate them and keep them as his unconscious pets. He liked their genitals and skulls as souvenirs.

Though I'm sure it's a terrible idea, Mom always says its polite
to accept an invitation. I bring cookies in saranwrap.
They're store-bought, but it's better to lie about these things.

His grandmother greets me and lets me in.
As we walk through the house, we chat
about the chocolate factory down their street,

how we both love chocolate, though I'm hypoglycemic and
can't eat sugar without passing out, but it's nice to agree
with a host. In the dining room, we find Jeffrey

setting at the table what he calls his "famous stew"
and before I can ask why it's famous, he's back in
the kitchen. I sit and look around the room.

His grandmother directs me to their art, a collection
of taxidermied heads displayed on the walls.
She brags how Jeffrey picked each boy out himself,

says she paid extra to have the best guy in town,
because taxidermy is both a science and an art.
I tell her the word comes from Greek meaning

"movement" and "skin" because that's all I know
about taxidermy, and it's always polite to add
to a conversation. I recognize a guy I dated,

and am relieved to understand why he never
called me back. Jeffrey has returned with a fistful
of knives. He carefully lays them down, lining up

tallest to sharpest, asks which one I prefer. Because it's always best to come prepared, I start digging

into my purse, tell him no thanks, I brought my own.

I put her back under my floor

Because it wasn't the strangest thing,
finding a dead girl beneath my kitchen.
Because her smallness discomforted me.
She was no bigger than my cat
though my cat is admittedly big.
Because the museum man wanted
22 thousand dollars. Because even
the funeral parlor wouldn't take her
for less than 7.
Because her coffin had a little window.
Because when I looked inside,
after a rag and some Windex,
there was nothing but dust, bone, hair,
all soft and matted together.
Because I wanted someone to talk to
while I did the dishes.
Because I guessed her hair
would've been wavy, like mine,
or that she laughed at serious things,
hated, too, sharing her food.
Because I never got along with children.
Because my cat was already jealous,
and my plate was much too heavy,
and the ground is where
we go to pray, which I assume means
it would make her
a better home.

the grim sleeper takes me hiking before his execution

Taking off more than a decade between killings, Lonnie David Franklin, Jr. was convicted in 2016 for the murders of 10 women. On August 10th, the LA court issued 10 death sentences—one for each victim.

You've decided to lead the way,
because you want to offer me
one last thing. I think that
if I was a good woman,
I'd protect you from this—
for doesn't love require suffering?

I look around to see our path
dug in from other sinners,
everyone seems to mistake
this steep hill for salvation.
I've decided, no, this is hell,
and drop back further.
your sweaty burnt skin, dirt clouds
from dirt rocks you kick up, only
to watch them explode in the air.

And because your back is turned,
I've slipped away,
not knowing how to say
this is your burden, your reparation,
your plate. This is something
I won't share.

perspective

We're sitting at her coffee table not talking,
surrounded by piles of newspapers, psychology books,
bibles with foreign titles, and she finally says,
What is that thing on your face?
A piercing, I tell her.
*Don't you have confidence
in your natural appeal?*
She says it must come from the parent tapes
playing in my head. *Your mother
has been infecting your brain for years, dear.*
Then about how my parent tapes
eat at my adult tapes, how routine is the devil's work.
She asks what dimension I've been living in,
because there are twelve, maybe more.
*Dear, expecting everyone to share the same reality
is ridiculous.* She tells me how attractive she was
at my age, recalls the many men who followed her,
who fought for her hand. *I never had any trouble
being natural,* she says. Now, jumping up as if
she just remembered the stove was on,
she rushes to a cluttered desk and pulls out
some dark, red dice with uneven sides.
They're future telling. Ask them a question.
I don't know what to say.
Go on. I still can't think of anything,
so she suggests I ask about a boy,
perhaps one I like. I tell her there is no boy.
Laughing, she waves her hand never mind,
and offers a cup of tea, leaving the room
before I can agree. After a few minutes,
I wonder if I have time to use the bathroom,
but then she returns with a painting in
her arms, marveling about its colors.
She asks about my color, says every soul
has a color. Hers is blue. *Blue to the core.
You can read all about it. I have
a book somewhere and you'll see.*

She says my mother is yellow,
which explains why they never get along.
When I don't respond, she frowns,
saying, *Dear, I'm beginning to worry.*
I can see indifference darkening your aura.
I smile and hand her my card because, really,
I was just stopping by to say happy birthday.
She's 77 now, though she prefers
going-on-78.
That's the only way to live, she says,
with perspective.

**sunday morning slasher dies on a friday, my letter doesn't arrive
'til monday**

*"When they asked him why he tried to kill the women, he told them that they had 'evil eyes'
and he wanted to 'release their spirits.' During further questioning, detectives were shocked
to hear that Coral claimed responsibility for up to 80 murders."*
      -Article on Carl "Coral" Eugene Watts

He liked me to call him Coral, liked the way it slowed
down my syllables, and he always preferred things slow.

That's why he did what he did. He wrote me that each murder
made his belly feel slow, and warm, like he'd drank too much,

made everything soft around him, even the body that lay at his feet.
He tried to explain them to me, his women. In one letter, Coral said

he did it for me, for us all, that these women were destined for great evil,
and it wasn't his fault that no one else could see it. I said I did, or that

I would try to, because Coral and me were fated, even if he scared me.
Some woman once said you should do the things that scare you.

When you're afraid, life gets bigger. Like when he'd ask me
to describe how the light hits my eyes, how much death they see.

I tried to warn him he was dying. I could hear it in the dryness of
his palms, how everything in jail moved too fast. If he'd gotten my letter,

he would've known it wasn't the cancer killing him. It was
his stomach—his heart—frozen and shrinking and emptied.

your friendly female anthropologist's take on bar pick-ups

The plan is
copulatory stare-gaze,
is chest thrust,
crouch and loom.
The plan is head tilt and blink,
wide-eyed, snouty jawed,
is three seconds
then look away,
is intently fiddle with your sweater.

The plan is to show interest.
Watch for the lip smack,
his ultimate sign of *hello there.*
Expose your upper teeth,
toss your hair, begin the contract.

The plan is to embellish simple gestures.
He'll stir his whiskey violently,
to show strength, then you will respond
by stomping your heels.

The plan is approach.
The plan is humming, soft voices.
Plan to amiably dominate his brain.
Land the casual arm graze.
Mirror his body language.
This will establish
the courting connection.
Lift your glass when he lifts.
Plan to synchronize
the stroking of your chins.

Be on guard.
He might try to talk politics
or play the air drums. No matter,
the plan is to act impressed,
because impressed-ness

is provocative.
The plan is to find each other's beat.
This beat is a ritual.
A genomic dance
passed down the human chain.

When the plan has reached
its culmination,
take him from the bar
with your arms at his waist
to subliminalize your claim
amongst the other females.
If another does manage
to lock in on your claim,
stand your ground—

or call it a day, because
that pizza next door
smells delicious.

bucket list

I want to give something that hurts,
just like Gandhi, or Buddha,
or Mayor Bloomberg.
I want to pretend I've been lost
in the woods. I want people
to believe the bear attacks I survived
and the trees that I felled. I want to order
for the man waiting next to me
in line at Starbucks, who is helplessly
reading and rereading the menu,
as if he's never heard of mocha Frappuccinos
or ancient grain flatbreads.
I want to move to Lake Charles, Louisiana,
the kind of place where people take notice
of new neighbors but are apprehensive
to greet them. I want to clip your weight.
I want to take scissors to my anger,
and watch you drift away.
I want to never drink again.
I want thirst to be a waste of time.
I want to figure out if my apartment building
has an office. I want to see if it contains happiness.
I want my body to grow like a river,
narrow, then wide, then endlessly.

losing weight

Five pounds:
I began ignoring mirrors after
Thoreau appeared one night,
urging me to gnaw at my bones.
You'll love it, he said,
lightly touching my neck.
My spine scuttled in his hands.

Ten pounds:
Now my dog leaves the room
when I walk in.
He's hurt.
He misses the way
I'd rub his chin
and let him lick the spoon.

Fifteen pounds:
In an infomercial,
God said he'd show me how
to give up perfection
and love myself
for only three easy payments
of $29.95.
I didn't want to believe
my body is a thing.

Thirty pounds:
I saw Moses in my bed.
He parted the sheets, asked
which side I preferred.
So I rolled over and will continue to do so
until he tells me I'm finished,
or until it's morning.

Fifty pounds:
The world got bigger.
The Buddha said it would,

that it needed to
before he could show me how
to plant the good seeds, how to eat
the good fruit.

Acknowledgements

"Why We Aren't Animals" published in *Gingerbread House Literary Magazine*

Previous version of "Skinned" published in *The Lonely Whale Anthology* by Chatsworth Press

"Losing Weight" published in *The Adirondack Review*

"Naked" published in *Poetry Quarterly*

"At a Party, John Wayne Gacy Puts his Arm around Me and Says We've all Been There Before" published in *491 Magazine*

"Someone Sets me up with Charles Manson", "The French Ripper Takes me to a Hot Dog Stand", and "Jeffrey Dahmer Invites me to a Dinner Party" published in *Fourth & Sycamore*

"Sunday Morning Slasher Dies on a Friday, My Letter Doesn't Arrive til Monday" published in *Thick With Conviction*

"Pair Bonds" published in *The Lake*
Previous version of "Perspective" published in *Dos Passos Review*

"Specimen" published in *Borfski Press*

Previous version of "Parasomnia" published in *Sonic Boom Journal*

"Reasoning with the Baby I Never Plan to Have" published in *Gravel Magazine*

"Pack" published in *Inklette Magazine*

"Bucket List" published in *Caravel Literary Arts Journal*

Previous version of "On Learning I am the Bully" published in *The Best of Kindness Anthology* by Origami Poems Project

"I put her back under my floor" published in *Door is a Jar Magazine*

Previous version of "Floating, Sinking" published in *BlazeVOX*

"The Angel Makers and I Try to Bake a Cake" published in *Words Dance Publishing*

"On Leaving the Green River Killer" published in *Dying Dahlia Review*

Previous version of "Your Friendly Female Anthropologist's Take On Bar Pick-Ups" published in *Adanna Literary Journal*

"The Grim Sleeper Takes me Hiking Before his Execution" published in *Helios Quarterly*

Bryanna Licciardi resists the question, "Where are you from?" She has lived all over the country—California, Texas, Michigan, Massachussetts, Louisiana—and currently resides just outside of Nashville, Tennessee. She received her BA in English from Austin Peay State University and her MFA in Poetry from Emerson College. Currently, she's studying literacy in a doctoral program at Middle Tennessee State University, where she also works as an academic advisor. When she's not working on a new diet plan for her overweight cat, Bryanna writes poetry, fiction, essays and lectures. Her work has appeared or is forthcoming in such publications as *BlazeVOX, Cleaver Magazine, Poetry Quarterly, Adirondack Review, Study.com*, and *Luna Luna*. More information about her work can be found at www.bryannalicciardi.com.

www.ingramcontent.com/pod-product-compliance
Lightning Source LLC
LaVergne TN
LVHW041603070426
835507LV00011B/1286